Hope Glen Rock fans
enjoy reading this
Book by a hometown author.

Michael E Jordan —

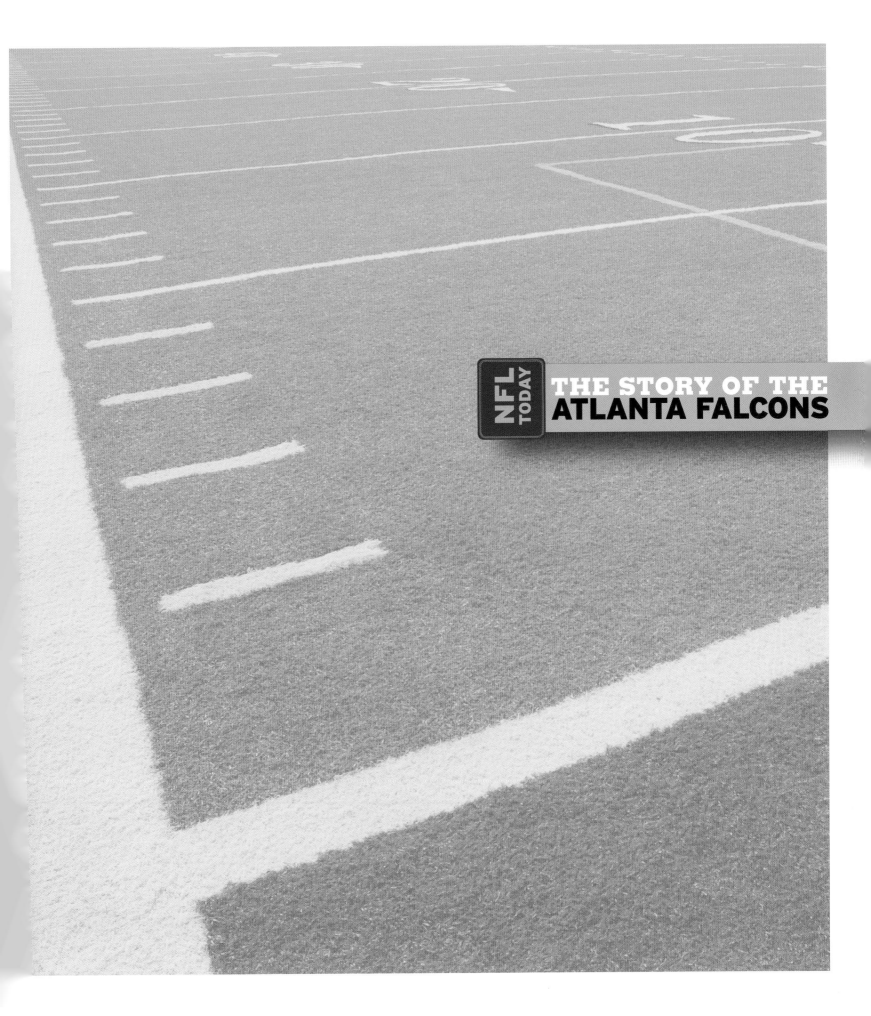

NFL TODAY

THE STORY OF THE
ATLANTA FALCONS

THE STORY OF THE ATLANTA FALCONS

MICHAEL E. GOODMAN

CREATIVE EDUCATION

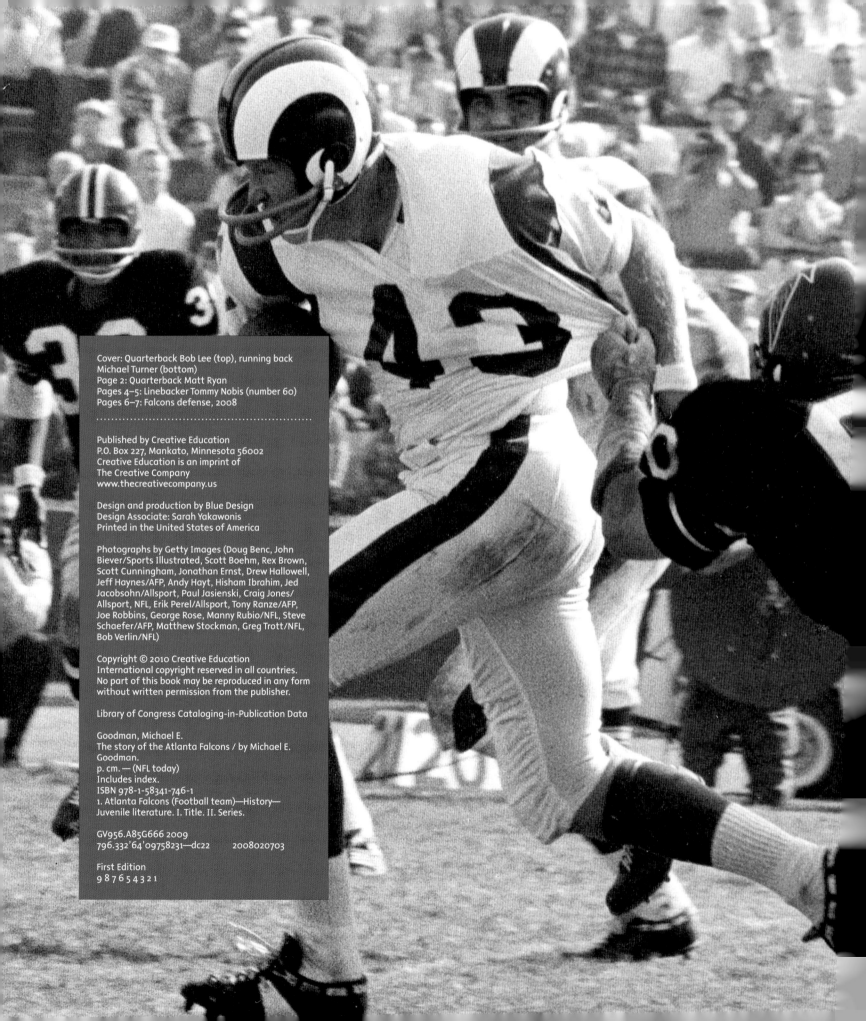

Cover: Quarterback Bob Lee (top), running back
Michael Turner (bottom)
Page 2: Quarterback Matt Ryan
Pages 4–5: Linebacker Tommy Nobis (number 60)
Pages 6–7: Falcons defense, 2008

....

Published by Creative Education
P.O. Box 227, Mankato, Minnesota 56002
Creative Education is an imprint of
The Creative Company
www.thecreativecompany.us

Design and production by Blue Design
Design Associate: Sarah Yakawonis
Printed in the United States of America

Photographs by Getty Images (Doug Benc, John
Biever/Sports Illustrated, Scott Boehm, Rex Brown,
Scott Cunningham, Jonathan Ernst, Drew Hallowell,
Jeff Haynes/AFP, Andy Hayt, Hisham Ibrahim, Jed
Jacobsohn/Allsport, Paul Jasienski, Craig Jones/
Allsport, NFL, Erik Perel/Allsport, Tony Ranze/AFP,
Joe Robbins, George Rose, Manny Rubio/NFL, Steve
Schaefer/AFP, Matthew Stockman, Greg Trott/NFL,
Bob Verlin/NFL)

Library of Congress Cataloging-in-Publication Data

Goodman, Michael E.
The story of the Atlanta Falcons / by Michael E.
Goodman.
p. cm. — (NFL today)
Includes index.
ISBN 978-1-58341-746-1
1. Atlanta Falcons (Football team)—History—
Juvenile literature. I. Title. II. Series.

GV956.A85G666 2009
796.332'64'09758231—dc22   2008020703

First Edition
9 8 7 6 5 4 3 2 1

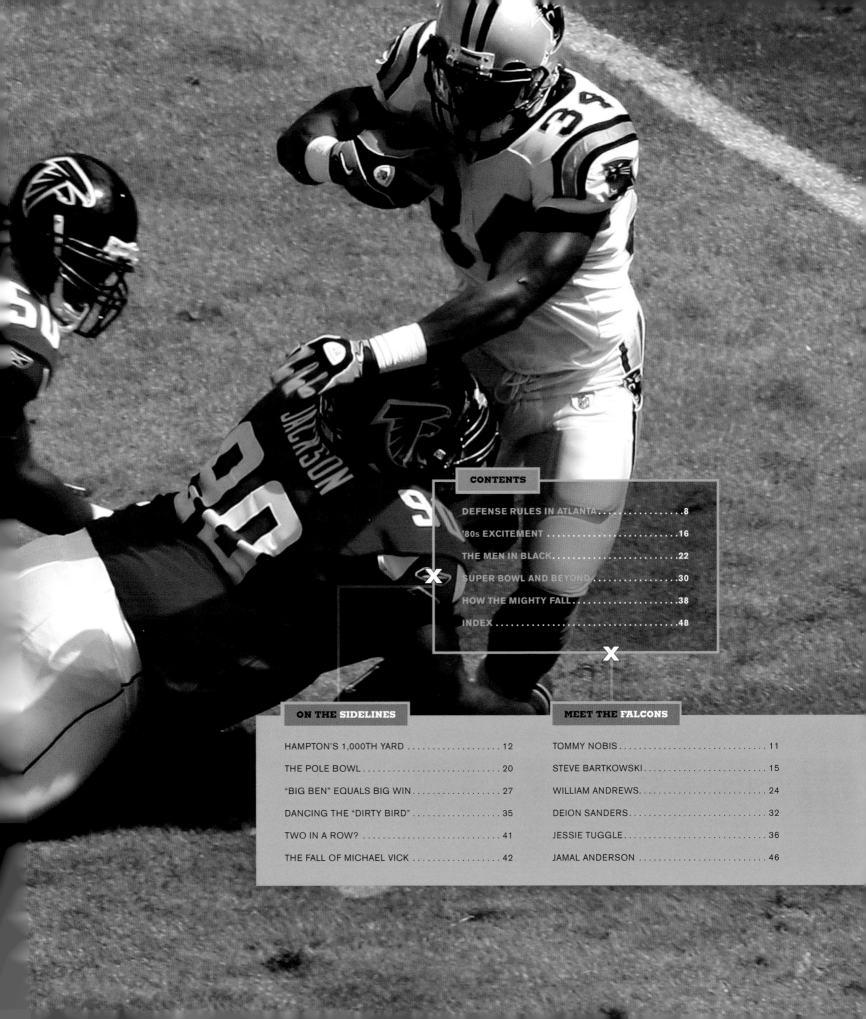

CONTENTS

ON THE SIDELINES

MEET THE FALCONS

DEFENSE RULES
IN ATLANTA

Atlanta, Georgia, is bustling. It is the fastest growing city in the United States, with the world's busiest airport, the Southeast's largest shopping mall, and one of the nation's newest and busiest rapid transit systems. It is also the birthplace of a wide range of businesses, from Coca-Cola to CNN. Atlanta began as a small railway connecting point in 1837 and, because of its strategic location, was burned to the ground by Union general William T. Sherman during the Civil War. Atlanta's citizens quickly began rebuilding their city, and by the 1900s, it had become the hub of commerce and culture in the Southeast.

In 1965, almost 100 years after Atlanta's rebuilding process had started, officials in the National Football League (NFL) chose the city to be the home of its first franchise in the Southeast. Team owners held a contest to name the new club, and a local schoolteacher submitted the winning entry, noting that "the falcon is proud and dignified, with great courage and fight." After taking the field for the first time, the Atlanta Falcons wasted no time in establishing a lasting football tradition in the South.

The Atlanta Falcons began play in 1966 as the 15th team in the NFL. The club was loaded with mediocre veterans and youngsters and was led by a rookie coach named Norb Hecker.

X Atlanta has long been an important transportation hub; railroads helped build the city up in the 1800s, and Atlanta's Hartsfield Airport is today one of the world's busiest.

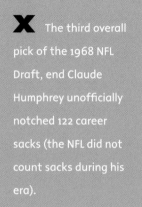

The Falcons didn't fly high in their first few years in the league, but they did feature a powerful defense led by hard-nosed linebacker Tommy Nobis, the first overall choice of the 1966 NFL Draft. The young star out of the University of Texas had a simple philosophy for playing effective defense. "I hit 'em right in the goozle—high and hard," he explained. "That way they don't go anywhere but down."

Unfortunately, Nobis couldn't play both defense and offense. The team's offensive squad—featuring quarterback Randy Johnson, running back Junior Coffey, and receiver Alex Hawkins—struggled all season. As a result, the low-scoring Falcons finished their first year with a 3–11 record.

After the club went an embarrassing 1–12–1 its second year, the Falcons changed coaches and drafted another defensive star. The new coach was former NFL quarterback

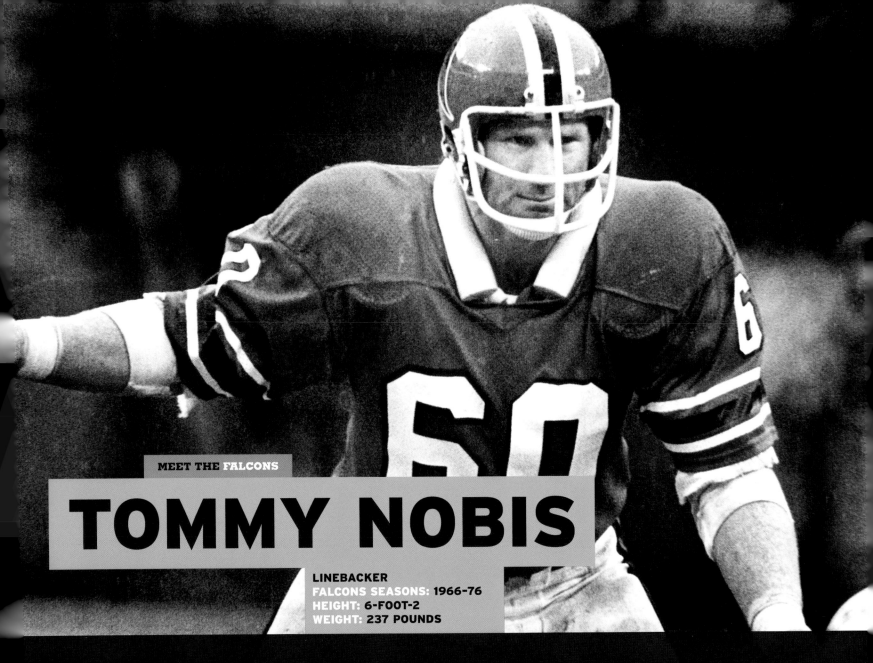

TOMMY NOBIS

LINEBACKER
FALCONS SEASONS: 1966–76
HEIGHT: 6-FOOT-2
WEIGHT: 237 POUNDS

Falcons team officials never had any question about which player the club should make its first-ever draft pick in 1966. Instead, the question was if Atlanta would be able to outmaneuver the Houston Oilers of the American Football League (AFL) to sign All-American linebacker Tommy Nobis from the University of Texas. Quick and aggressive, Nobis was the type of player a team could build its defense around—especially a young team such as the Falcons. Atlanta won the bidding war for Nobis and never regretted the decision, as he was named Defensive Rookie of the Year in 1966 and became the team's first Pro Bowl participant that year. Nobis played 11 years in Atlanta and was selected to the Pro Bowl in 5 of those seasons. He was later named to the NFL's "All-1960s" team. Nobis once explained his no-nonsense work ethic by saying, "A man ought to have enough pride to play every game as hard as he can, wringing every bit of energy he has in him trying to win. That's the only thing that matters in football."

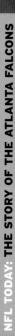
ON THE SIDELINES

HAMPTON'S 1,000TH YARD

The goal of every NFL running back is to rush for 1,000 yards in a season, but doing so requires hard work and a little bit of luck. In the final game of the 1972 season, Falcons halfback Dave Hampton was closing in on the 1,000-yard mark. Then, a hard run up the middle brought his total to exactly 1,000. The game was stopped, and officials presented Hampton with the game ball. Unfortunately, Hampton decided to try one more run. This time, he was thrown for a five-yard loss, dropping his total to 995 as the game ended. Hampton kept the game ball but lost the record. The next season, Hampton also came tantalizingly close, finishing the year with 997 yards. Two years later, Hampton went into the last game of the season only 59 yards shy of 1,000. He reached the elusive total late in the game on an off-tackle run that brought his total to 1,002 yards. This time, Hampton didn't test his luck. He willingly sat out the rest of the game and took his place in the Falcons' record book.

Norm Van Brocklin. The new defensive standout was end Claude Humphrey from Tennessee State University. Humphrey keyed a fierce Falcons pass rush and was named the NFL's Defensive Rookie of the Year in 1968.

Van Brocklin was a demanding and stubborn coach, and he had a stormy relationship with many of his players. Yet, little by little, the players adapted to his coaching methods, and the team's performance improved. Led by Nobis, Humphrey, end John Zook, and cornerback Ken Reaves, the defense battered opponents. In 1969, the Falcons finished 6–8, and in 1971, they recorded their first winning season (7–6–1). Still, the team's offense continued to sputter, and Van Brocklin's Falcons never became big winners.

Late in the 1974 season, Van Brocklin was fired and replaced by defensive coordinator Marion Campbell. Campbell, who had built the Atlanta defense, knew the club needed a leader on offense, too. Scouts for the team believed they knew just the person for the job: quarterback Steve Bartkowski at the University of California. The Falcons engineered a trade to gain the top pick in the NFL Draft, which they used to select Bartkowski.

Atlanta fans gave the blond Californian a warm welcome, and Bartkowski loved the attention. "I enjoyed picking up the paper and reading that I was the team's savior," he said. "I really thought I could walk in here and turn the team around overnight." However, injuries and mistakes slowed Bartkowski's rise to stardom, as did his tendency to party late into the night. He had trouble adjusting to pro defenses and suffered through a 4–10 rookie season. Then he missed much of the following two seasons with knee injuries. In 1978, Bartkowski returned healthy, but miserable preseason performances led new coach Leeman Bennett to bench the young quarterback. "That was the lowest I've ever been in my life," Bartkowski later recalled, "and it was also the best thing that ever happened to me."

Bartkowski gave up partying and refocused his life. He regained the starting position early in the 1978 season and—with the help of receivers Wallace Francis and Alfred Jenkins—led the team to a five-game winning streak. The Falcons finished 9–7 and made the playoffs for the first time in their history. After Atlanta beat the Philadelphia Eagles 14–13 in the first round, Falcons fans began dreaming of a Super Bowl. But the Dallas Cowboys gave them a rude awakening the following week, defeating Atlanta 27–20 and eliminating the team from the playoffs.

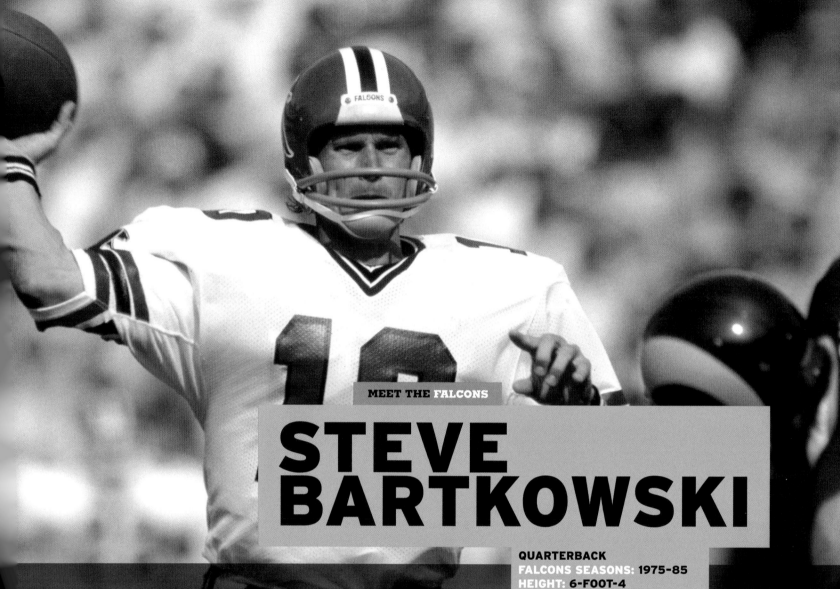

STEVE BARTKOWSKI

QUARTERBACK
FALCONS SEASONS: 1975-85
HEIGHT: 6-FOOT-4
WEIGHT: 213 POUNDS

For their first nine seasons, the Falcons were known for their hard-hitting defense and their anemic offense. To turn that trend around, the club made Steve Bartkowski its number-one overall pick in the 1975 NFL Draft. Blessed with confidence and a rocket arm, the tall Californian quickly established himself as the team's leader. "The guys just seem to flock around him, and he responds," said coach Marion Campbell. "He provides the spark this team needs to win. Steve's not the tough-guy type. He's more liable to say, 'Just give me one more second, guys, and I'll get that pass in there.' They believe he can do it, so they give him that one more second." Bartkowski was named NFL Rookie of the Year by *Pro Football Weekly* in 1975, beating out future Hall-of-Famers Randy White of the Dallas Cowboys and Walter Payton of the Chicago Bears. Over his 11-year career in Atlanta, Bartkowski went to 2 Pro Bowls and led the NFL in touchdown passes once—in 1980, when he piloted Atlanta to its first National Football Conference (NFC) West Division title.

'80S
EXCITEMENT

X------

The Atlanta offense got a boost the next season with the

arrival of hard-driving running back William Andrews from

Auburn University. Andrews simply overpowered tacklers,

rushing for more than 1,000 yards in his rookie season. He

achieved success with a unique style, running slightly bent over

with his head lowered. "I try to stay lower than my opponent,"

Andrews explained, "come at him in a ball, and then ... POW!"

By 1980, the Falcons were ready for a run at a

championship. That season, Andrews, Bartkowski, and Jenkins

set new team records for rushing, passing, and pass receiving

respectively. The club went 12–4 and won its first NFC West

Division title. In the playoffs, the Falcons once again faced off

against the Cowboys in front of the largest crowd in Atlanta-

Fulton County Stadium history. Atlanta led 27–17 in the fourth

quarter, but Dallas rallied to hand the Falcons a crushing

30–27 defeat.

After beginning the decade on a high note, the Falcons

slipped toward the bottom of the NFC West. While the team

fell in the standings, Andrews continued to rise, making the Pro Bowl four years in a row from 1980 to 1983. Then, in a preseason scrimmage in August 1984, Andrews was tackled from behind, and something snapped in his knee. The devastating injury put him on the sidelines for two seasons. Andrews tried to make a comeback in 1986, but the damaged knee wasn't strong enough for him to keep playing. Luckily for the team, Andrews's backup, bruising running back Gerald Riggs, took over the starting role and went on to surpass Andrews in the Falcons' record books by averaging nearly 1,000 rushing yards per season between 1982 and 1988.

Another Atlanta favorite in the 1980s was wide receiver and kick returner Billy "White Shoes" Johnson, who was known for his lightning speed and fancy footwear. Opponents hated watching those white cleats race by in a blur when Johnson returned punts and kickoffs for the Falcons. They also hated the dance he would do in the end zone to celebrate any touchdown he scored.

Despite the presence of such stars, the Falcons continued to post losing records for the rest of the 1980s. Then, late in the decade, they began rebuilding around two key draft picks: quarterback Chris Miller from the University of Oregon and cornerback Deion Sanders from Florida State University. A long-range bomber, Miller combined with receivers Andre Rison and Michael Haynes to give the Falcons one of the most fearsome

Although best known for his electrifying punt returns, Billy Johnson was also a valuable receiver; in 1985, at age 33, he set career bests with 830 receiving yards and 5 touchdowns. **X**

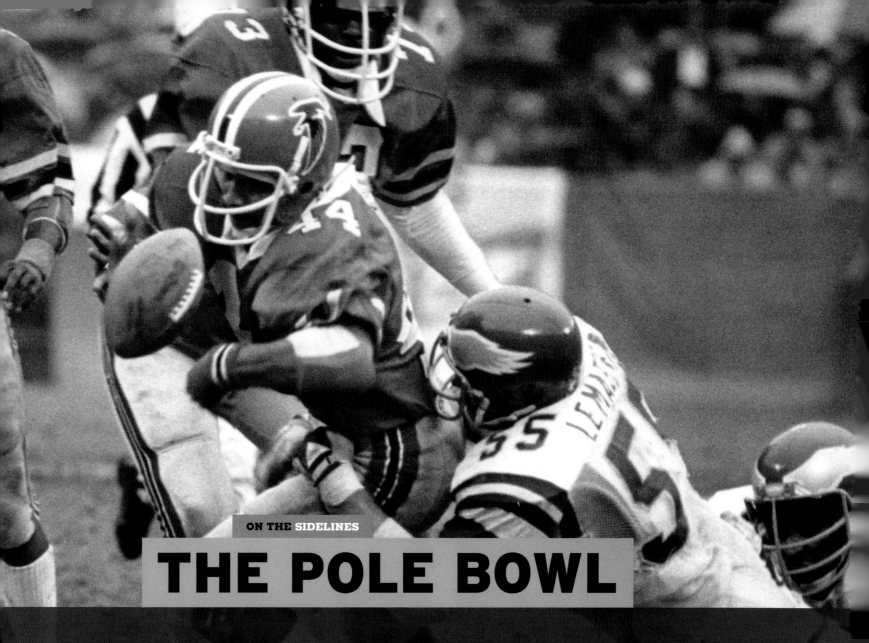

THE POLE BOWL

Atlanta fans received an early Christmas present on December 24, 1978, when the Falcons took on the Philadelphia Eagles in Atlanta-Fulton County Stadium in their first-ever playoff game. The fans, who had been eagerly anticipating a Falcons postseason game since 1966, cheered excitedly in the rainy, 40-degree weather. The crowd quieted down considerably in the third quarter when Philadelphia moved out to a 13–0 lead, but it perked up again as quarterback Steve Bartkowski led the Falcons on a fourth-quarter charge. Bartkowski completed touchdown passes to tight end Jim Mitchell and wide receiver Wallace Francis in the last five minutes to engineer a 14–13 Atlanta victory. As the gun sounded to end the game, thousands of fans poured onto the field, mobbing the players and tearing down the goalposts. Because of the wild celebration, the game became known as "The Pole Bowl." Falcons linebacker Greg Brezina, who was in the middle of the mob, said, "Those fans hit me harder than the Eagles did. But they deserved to be on the field. They've waited 13 years for this."

passing attacks in the league. Meanwhile, Sanders quickly became famous for shutting down opposing receivers with his blanket coverage.

The Falcons faced a challenge in signing Sanders, whose flashy moves as a cornerback and kick returner had earned him the nicknames "Neon Deion" and "Prime Time." The versatile athlete was also a top baseball player for the New York Yankees. Both franchises wanted Sanders's full-time services, but he had a different plan in mind. Sanders figured he could play both sports—baseball in the summer and football in the fall.

Sanders put his plan into action in 1989. He played baseball most of the summer for the Yankees and then reported to Falcons training camp two days before the season opener. Even without much practice, Prime Time was electric in his first Falcons game, breaking tackles and outrunning opponents on a 68-yard punt return for a touchdown. Atlanta fans were delirious with excitement, and even coach Marion Campbell was impressed. "In my 27 years in the league, I've never experienced the buzz that goes through a stadium as when this guy gets near the football," he said.

THE MEN IN
BLACK

The Falcons opened the 1990s displaying the talents of young stars such as Miller, Sanders, and Rison. They also had an eccentric new coach in Jerry Glanville. Glanville was brought in to shake things up in Atlanta, and he delivered. First, he changed the team's jerseys from red to black. Then he changed the club's attitude, installing a high-powered "Red Gun" passing offense developed by assistant coach June Jones—a former Falcons quarterback—and building an aggressive defense around linebacker Jessie Tuggle.

In 1991, the team adopted hip-hop star MC Hammer's "2 Legit 2 Quit" as its rallying cry. Taking a cue from the song, the Falcons wouldn't quit all season. They staged several exciting comebacks and stormed into the playoffs with a 10–6 record. Then they topped off the season by earning a dramatic comeback in a first-round playoff game against the New Orleans Saints. In that game, Miller connected with Haynes for a 61-yard touchdown strike that turned a late-game deficit into a 27–20 Atlanta victory. It was the Falcons' first

Known as a colorful character who could be humorous one moment and combative the next, coach Jerry Glanville was always good for a clever quote—or an argument with referees.

[22]

X

WILLIAM ANDREWS

RUNNING BACK
FALCONS SEASONS: 1979-86
HEIGHT: 6 FEET
WEIGHT: 210 POUNDS

In his first five seasons in the NFL (1979–83), William Andrews was the best all-around running back in the league. He was named to the Pro Bowl four of those years and quickly became the Falcons' all-time leading rusher. Andrews was also an excellent receiver, and he twice gained more than 2,000 total (rushing and receiving) yards in a year. Andrews's strength and balance made it almost impossible for a single defender to bring him down. Hall of Fame safety Ronnie Lott of the San Francisco 49ers described one attempt he made to tackle Andrews: "I ran 10 yards straight at him, as hard as I could," Lott told a *Sports Illustrated* writer. "Then, boom. I slid off of him like butter. I hit the ground, and he didn't go down. I was thinking, 'What happened?'" What finally did stop Andrews was a terrible knee injury that cut short his career in 1984. In 2004, Andrews was honored with induction into the Falcons' Ring of Honor in the Georgia Dome, a tribute to retired players who made significant contributions to the team.

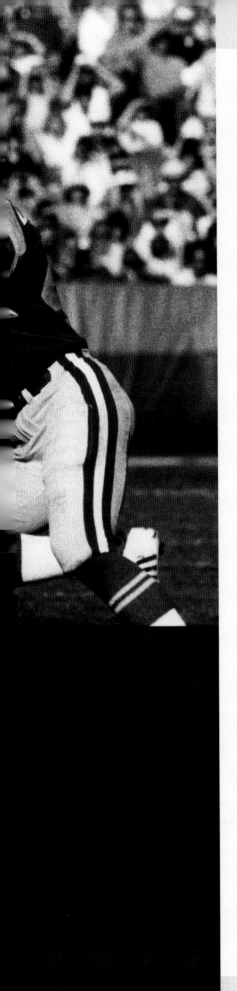

playoff win in 13 years. Although the Falcons were eliminated from the postseason the following week by the eventual Super Bowl champion Washington Redskins, Glanville's team woke up Atlanta fans.

The next season, the Falcons moved into a new home: Atlanta's giant Georgia Dome. Playing before record-breaking home crowds, the Falcons stumbled to two straight 6–10 seasons before Glanville was fired and replaced by June Jones. Jones designed a new offense around the passing combination of quarterback Jeff George and wide receiver Terance Mathis. This pairing resulted in a team record, as Mathis caught 111 passes in 1994.

Optimism was high in Atlanta in 1995, especially when the team got off to a quick 5–2 start. Led by George, Mathis, and running back Craig "Ironhead" Heyward (known for his habit of charging forward with his head down), the team's offense was outstanding. George became the first Atlanta quarterback to top the prestigious 4,000-yard mark in passing, while Heyward gained 1,083 yards on the ground. Despite fading in the second half of the season, the Falcons made the playoffs with a 9–7 record, only to lose in the opening round of the postseason to the Green Bay Packers.

Fortunately for Atlanta fans, positive change was coming.

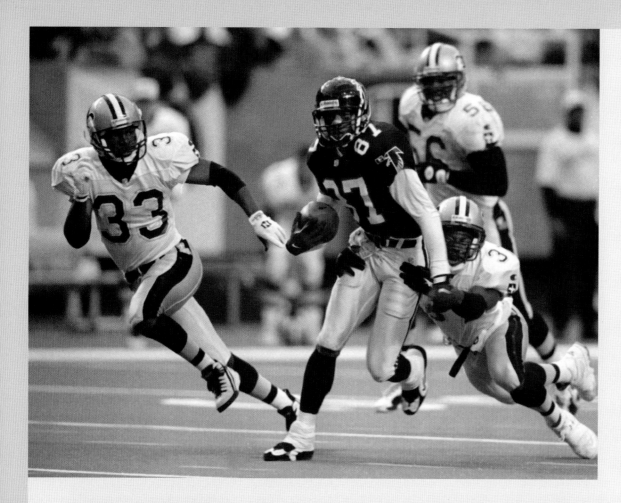

X Bert Emanuel averaged nearly 1,000 receiving yards a season during his 4 years in Atlanta and scored a career-high 9 touchdowns in 1997.

In January 1997, the Falcons replaced Jones with Dan Reeves, who had previously coached the Denver Broncos to three Super Bowl appearances in the 1980s. Reeves's hiring excited both Atlanta fans and players. "He's a winner," said Falcons defensive end Chuck Smith, "and he knows what it takes to get it done in this league."

One of Coach Reeves's first moves was to acquire veteran quarterback Chris Chandler from the Houston Oilers to provide much-needed experience and leadership. Chandler combined with running back Jamal Anderson and wide receiver Bert Emanuel to establish a smooth-running offense in Atlanta. But in 1997, the Falcons' defensive line made an

"BIG BEN" EQUALS BIG WIN

In 1991, the Falcons made comeback after comeback to record their first winning season in nine years. The most exciting Atlanta victory, a 17–14 last-second triumph over the San Francisco 49ers, came via a trick play the team hadn't used successfully for 13 years. It was called "Big Ben Right," a variation of what is sometimes called a "Hail Mary" pass. To execute the play, several receivers race toward the end zone, and the quarterback throws the ball as far as he can. Receivers and defenders battle for the ball on what is usually a game-deciding play. In 1978, quarterback Steve Bartkowski won two games for the Falcons with Big Ben Right passes. Those two victories helped the Falcons reach the playoffs for the first time in their history. In the 1991 game against San Francisco, backup quarterback Billy Joe Tolliver (pictured) executed Big Ben Right perfectly for a 44-yard game-winning pass to receiver Michael Haynes. Because both Atlanta and San Francisco had finished the season with identical 10–6 records, the win enabled the Falcons to beat out the 49ers for a playoff berth.

X Speedy and brash, cornerback Ray Buchanan established himself as one of the NFL's top ballhawks by making 27 interceptions from 1997 to 2001.

even more remarkable turnaround, as it set a club record for quarterback sacks with 55. Such achievements left the Falcons and their fans brimming with confidence. "It's time to stand up and be counted," announced cornerback Ray Buchanan. "No more rebuilding and moral victories. It's time to get it done."

X Quarterback Chris Chandler brought a wealth of experience to Atlanta in 1997, having already suited up for five different NFL teams.

X----------

The patience of Falcons fans was finally rewarded in 1998 as the club romped to a 14–2 record and the top spot in the NFC West. Behind Anderson's strong running and Chandler's pinpoint passing, the Falcons' offense pounded opposing defenses. Anderson also set an NFL record with 410 carries and a club record with 1,846 rushing yards. Meanwhile, the defense, led by linebackers Jessie Tuggle and Cornelius Bennett, ranked near the top of the NFC.

Tuggle described the magical season this way: "When we hit the field, a lot of veteran leadership took over, and we felt like we couldn't lose. Sometimes you have a team—it may not be the most talented team—but when you believe in yourself and fight for one goal and become one unit, then great things happen for you. That's what happened to us. We got a little confidence. We took that confidence and mixed in some pretty good ability, and we went a long way."

In the postseason, Atlanta edged past San Francisco 20–18 to reach the NFC Championship Game against the 15–1 Minnesota Vikings. Playing in Minnesota's Metrodome, the two teams fought to a 27–27 tie in regulation and then kept battling into overtime. Atlanta's defense twice stopped the powerful Vikings offense before the Falcons won the game on a field goal by kicker Morten Andersen. The once lowly Falcons

X Thanks in part to a fast and aggressive defense that ranked fourth in the NFL, the Falcons were unbeatable in 1998 when playing inside the noisy Georgia Dome.

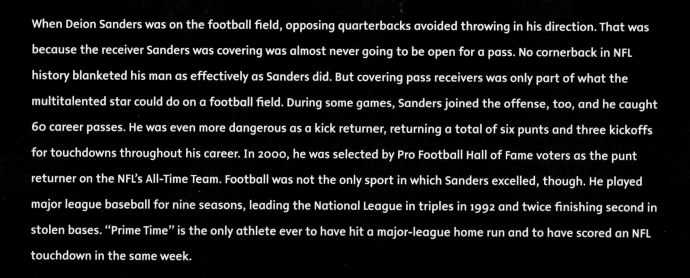

DEION SANDERS

CORNERBACK
FALCONS SEASONS: 1989-93
HEIGHT: 6-FOOT-1
WEIGHT: 198 POUNDS

When Deion Sanders was on the football field, opposing quarterbacks avoided throwing in his direction. That was because the receiver Sanders was covering was almost never going to be open for a pass. No cornerback in NFL history blanketed his man as effectively as Sanders did. But covering pass receivers was only part of what the multitalented star could do on a football field. During some games, Sanders joined the offense, too, and he caught 60 career passes. He was even more dangerous as a kick returner, returning a total of six punts and three kickoffs for touchdowns throughout his career. In 2000, he was selected by Pro Football Hall of Fame voters as the punt returner on the NFL's All-Time Team. Football was not the only sport in which Sanders excelled, though. He played major league baseball for nine seasons, leading the National League in triples in 1992 and twice finishing second in stolen bases. "Prime Time" is the only athlete ever to have hit a major-league home run and to have scored an NFL touchdown in the same week.

were bound for the Super Bowl at last. One jubilant fan
watching the game on television in Atlanta remarked, "There
are two things I never thought I would say together: 'Atlanta
Falcons' and 'Super Bowl.'"

In the Super Bowl against the defending champion
Denver Broncos, the Falcons jumped out to a 3–0 lead five
minutes into the game. But the Atlanta defense could
not restrain Denver quarterback John Elway, who directed
a Broncos attack that totaled more than 450 yards. The

X Linebacker
Cornelius Bennett
played in five Super
Bowls (four with the
Buffalo Bills and one
with Atlanta) but was
on the losing side
every time.

final result was a 34–19 Denver win that ended Atlanta's championship dreams.

The Falcons followed up their Super Bowl season with two disappointing years. Coach Reeves knew that the team needed new blood, so he engineered a trade with the San Diego Chargers to obtain the top pick in the 2001 NFL Draft. The Falcons used the opportunity to select Michael Vick, a multidimensional quarterback who had excelled as both a passer and a runner during his college career at Virginia Tech.

Vick's arrival signaled a new era for Atlanta. In 2002, or the first time in 10 years, all 8 of the team's home games were sellouts, as fans packed the Georgia Dome to see the new, highflying Falcons. Vick quickly blossomed into one of the NFL's most exciting stars, passing for nearly 3,000 yards and rushing for 777 more in his rookie season. Other offensive stars that year included halfback Warrick Dunn and second-year tight end Alge Crumpler. Together, they propelled Atlanta back into the postseason.

Describing Vick's play, sportswriter Mike Holbrook noted, "He has shown a penchant for doing the impossible and producing at least one play that leaves you saying, 'That's impossible,' or 'I've never seen that before.' He's the closest

DANCING THE "DIRTY BIRD"

Falcons players and fans had a lot to celebrate in 1998—the year Atlanta reached the Super Bowl—but no one celebrated more flamboyantly than running back Jamal Anderson. It was not only his running and pass catching but also his dancing that enabled Anderson to make team history that year. Each time he scored a touchdown (which happened 16 times during the regular season and 3 more times in the playoffs), Anderson would perform a dance he called the "Dirty Bird." Soon, fans began doing the dance in the stands after Atlanta touchdowns, and coach Dan Reeves even performed it on the field in Minnesota after the Falcons defeated the Vikings in the NFC title game. How does one do the "Dirty Bird"? First, you lift your right arm in the air, then bring the arm down across your chest to form a wing. Then do the same actions with your left arm. Next, flap your arms as if you're trying to fly. "Then you do whatever you feel like," said Anderson. Doing the Dirty Bird, the Falcons flew high in 1998.

JESSIE TUGGLE

LINEBACKER
FALCONS SEASONS: 1987–2000
HEIGHT: 5-FOOT-11
WEIGHT: 231 POUNDS

The Falcons didn't have to look far to find Jessie Tuggle. The tough, undersized linebacker grew up just 75 miles from Atlanta in Griffin, Georgia. Yet his joining the Falcons was really just a lucky break. The team didn't draft Tuggle following his graduation from Division II Valdosta State College in 1987; the Falcons signed him only as a favor to his college coach, giving him a $500 signing bonus. Yet Tuggle played his heart out in his first training camp and quickly earned the nickname "The Hammer" for his bone-jarring tackles. He impressed his coaches right away and cracked the starting lineup in his rookie year. Tuggle started 189 games from 1987 to 2000 and led the team in tackles during 10 of his 14 seasons in Atlanta. During those years, he was selected to the Pro Bowl five times. "Jessie Tuggle was the franchise," former Falcons cornerback Ray Buchanan once said. Tuggle's number 58 is one of 6 jerseys retired by the Falcons. It hangs proudly in the Falcons' Ring of Honor.

thing to a human highlight film as there is in the sport."

In the first round of the 2002 playoffs, Vick and the Falcons shocked football experts by handing the Green Bay Packers their first-ever playoff loss at Lambeau Field in wintry Wisconsin. However, they fell to the Philadelphia Eagles the next week, delaying their hopes of making a return to the Super Bowl.

Michael Vick was perhaps the most athletic NFL quarterback ever, strong-armed and able to run the 40-yard dash in 4.3 seconds. **X**

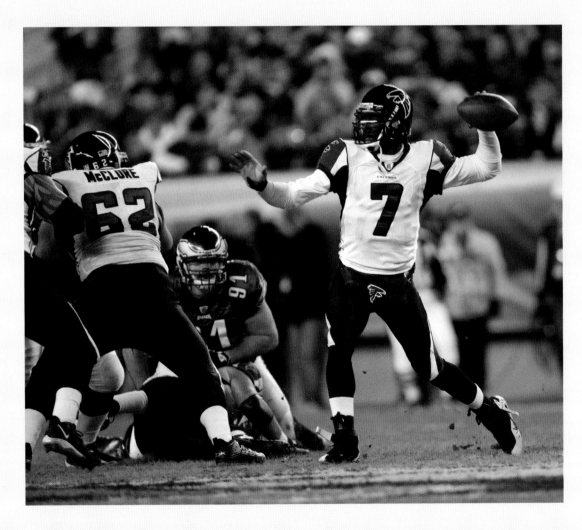

X ---------------

The Falcons literally got off on the wrong foot in 2003, as Vick suffered a broken leg during the preseason and missed most of the year. Atlanta fans got to see what they had missed when Vick made his first start late in the season and rushed for 141 yards—the third-highest total by a quarterback in NFL history—to lead the Falcons to a win over the Carolina Panthers. Nevertheless, as the team concluded a dismal 5–11 season, Coach Reeves was dismissed and replaced by Jim Mora Jr.

Mora immediately began rebuilding the team's offense around Vick and Crumpler and its defense around linebacker Keith Brooking and cornerback DeAngelo Hall. The club reversed its previous year's showing by going 11–5 to finish atop the NFC South (a new division formed in 2002). The Falcons then blew out the St. Louis Rams in the first round of the playoffs but came up short against the Philadelphia Eagles in the NFC Championship Game. Falcons players were disappointed that their season had ended so quickly. "I can look in my teammates' eyes and tell that we're not fully satisfied," said Brooking. "There is still a hunger inside of us, and that's what's so great about this team."

That hunger was visible during the first half of the 2005 season when the Falcons got off to a 6–2 start. However, the

X Linebacker Keith Brooking played his entire football career—from the Pee Wee level to the NFL—in his home state of Georgia; he joined the Falcons after attending college at Georgia Tech.

team then sputtered, finishing the season at 8–8 and out
of the playoffs. When the club suffered another late-season
collapse in 2006, Mora was fired and replaced by Bobby
Petrino from the University of Louisville.

Petrino was brought in primarily to rebuild the Falcons'
offense around Michael Vick. The new coach impressed
football experts with the high-power passing attack he had
developed at Louisville. "Bobby Petrino is a difference maker
who will bring a strong identity to the Falcons," declared
team owner Arthur Blank.

Unfortunately, Petrino never got the opportunity to work
with Vick. The superstar quarterback was arrested during
the summer of 2007 and charged with running an illegal
dogfighting ring in Virginia. The evidence disturbed most fans,
and many animal rights advocates marched in protest outside
the Georgia Dome. After pleading guilty, Vick was imprisoned
and suspended from the NFL, leaving his football career in
jeopardy. "What I did was immature, so it means I need to
grow up," Vick said in an interview before he went to jail. "I
hope that every young kid out there in the world watching
this interview … will use me as an example to using better
judgment and making better decisions."

Then, 14 weeks into the 2007 season, Petrino also left

ON THE SIDELINES
TWO IN A ROW?

On December 24, 2005, many Atlanta fans were hoping to receive a special gift. A Falcons win over the Tampa Bay Buccaneers that Saturday afternoon would allow the team to put together two winning seasons in a row, something it had never done in its 39-year history. Falcons fans were cautiously optimistic. The team had gotten off to a 6–2 start in 2005, but then strange things began to happen. Quarterback Michael Vick lost his passing touch, runners began to fumble, and tacklers began missing their men. Still, the team's record stood at 8–6 going into the Tampa Bay game, and one more victory would mean two winning seasons in a row. When running back T. J. Duckett scored with less than six minutes to go, putting Atlanta ahead 24–17, the celebrating began. But the Buccaneers fought back, tying the game in the final minute and winning it in overtime. The next week, Atlanta fans had little to celebrate on New Year's Day either, as the Carolina Panthers dismantled the Falcons 44–11, dooming the team to an 8–8 finish.

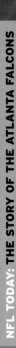
ON THE SIDELINES

THE FALL OF MICHAEL VICK

When the Falcons made Michael Vick the top overall pick in the 2001 NFL Draft, they knew they were getting a player who could do spectacular things on the field but could sometimes be a little out of control in his personal life. What they didn't know was that Vick had a dark secret: Vick and some friends had organized an illegal dogfighting and gambling enterprise. They set up a kennel on Vick's sprawling Virginia estate where they trained dogs to fight and then staged vicious battles between the animals. The existence of the dogfighting ring and Vick's involvement in it became big news in the summer of 2007. After several of the quarterback's partners pleaded guilty, Vick also agreed to a plea bargain and was sentenced to 23 months in jail. With Vick imprisoned, the Falcons lost one of the most exciting players in team history. But Vick lost far more, forfeiting much of the $130-million contract he had signed with Atlanta, many lucrative endorsement contracts, and the respect of thousands of fans. For the once highflying Vick, the fall was quick and costly.

the team to return to college coaching at the University of Arkansas. The Falcons replaced him with coach Mike Smith, who had helped construct an outstanding defense for the Jacksonville Jaguars. In his first press conference, Smith assured Falcons fans that there would be a brighter future in Atlanta. "There's nowhere to go but up," he said. "I'm not concerned with the past. I'm concerned with what's happening from today on."

That future arrived more quickly than anyone could have imagined. In 2008, behind the outstanding play of rookie quarterback Matt Ryan, running back Michael Turner, and standout pass rusher John Abraham, the Falcons soared to

X Although he was rarely the Falcons' starting running back, speedy Jerious Norwood led the NFL in yards-per-rush average in 2007.

X A 6-foot-4 receiver, Michael Jenkins (pictured) provided a big passing target first for Michael Vick, then, in 2008, for Matt Ryan.

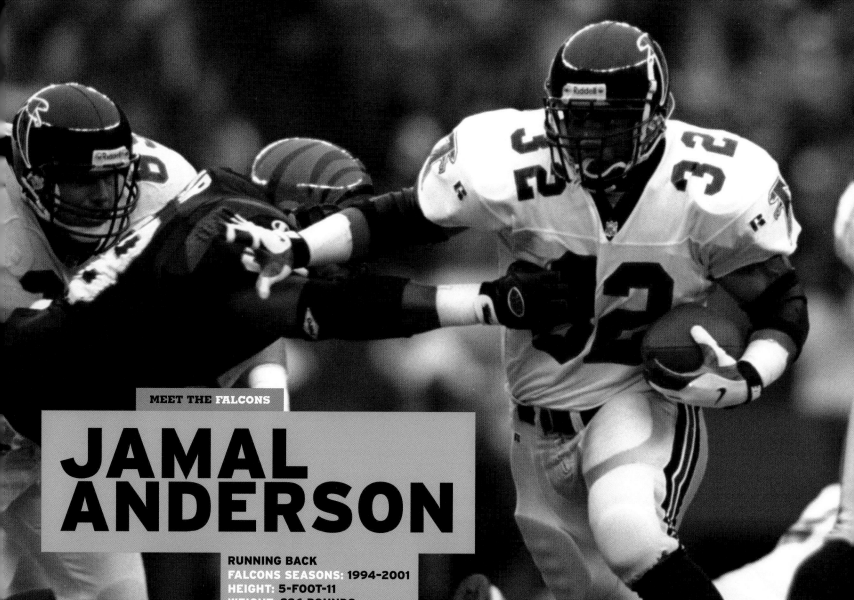

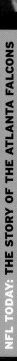

MEET THE FALCONS

JAMAL ANDERSON

RUNNING BACK
FALCONS SEASONS: 1994–2001
HEIGHT: 5-FOOT-11
WEIGHT: 236 POUNDS

Following his graduation from the University of Utah in 1994, Jamal Anderson was not high on any NFL scout's list. Most thought he was too big and slow to be a pro running back and too small to be a blocking fullback. The Falcons finally selected him in the seventh round of the 1994 NFL Draft, never expecting him to make the team. But Anderson was confident of his skills. "I'm not real fast, I'm not real quick—I can tell you a lot of things I'm not good at," Anderson said, "but I pride myself on being able to run you over, run around you, and make you miss. Every time you face me, you don't know what you're going to get. You may get a shoulder in the mouth, you may get a stiff-arm, you may get shook." It took several seasons for Anderson to become the Falcons' number-one running back, but his determination never wavered. His true talents emerged in 1998, when he pounded out nearly 1,850 yards on the field and carried the Falcons all the way to the Super Bowl.

a stunning 11–5 record and captured a Wild Card berth in the playoffs, announcing themselves as a fast-rising force in the NFC South.

For more than 40 years, the Atlanta Falcons have brought their fans a mixture of excitement and heartache. The team has struggled to find a winning touch, but it has also made some amazing comebacks over the years. Today's Falcons have the franchise's first Super Bowl trophy in their sights and plan to make this hub of the South the center of NFL glory soon.

INDEX